Problems with Plastic

Contents | Page

written by Samantha Montgomerie

Plastic is man-made. It is easy to make it into shapes, which is why we use it for many things.

We use it to make boxes, bottles, toys, and more.

plastic on our planet

When plastic goes into our oceans, it affects many animals. They eat the plastic thinking it is food.

The Pacific Garbage Patch shows us the problem we are making for our planet. The plastic in the ocean cannot break down.

The Pacific Garbage Patch

We need to find ways to reduce the plastic we use. We can choose to buy things that are not made of plastic.

We can reuse plastic in our homes. We can use it many times before we recycle it. We should reuse plastic boxes and bottles.

If we cannot reuse plastic, we should recycle it. It will be melted down and made into other things.

recycling plastic

We can start to help our planet by what we do at home.

We can start to wrap our lunch in cloth wraps. We can reuse plastic items. We can recycle plastic things and put them in a recycling bin.

We should show others how to recycle. We can teach our class at school to recycle. We can talk to them about using less plastic.

helping at school

We can do some things to fix the problems plastic has made. We can pick up plastic on the beach.

We need to teach others how to reduce, reuse, and recycle. This will help our planet and the animals that live on it.